Clay Play

Learning Games For Children

Clay Play

Learning Games For Children

by henry post and michael mctwigan

with notes for adults by mihalyi csikszentmihalyi,

committee on human development, university of chicago

illustrations by diane martin

prentice-hall, inc. englewood cliffs, n.j.

to henry/mm
to michael/hp

We wish to thank the children, teachers and parents
of the West Side Community Alliance Day Care Center
in New York City for their cheerful cooperation and
invaluable assistance in making this book what it is.
Special thanks to Ellen.

Photos by Jon Atkin

Printed in the United States of America

Prentice-Hall International, Inc., London
Prentice-Hall of Australia, Pty. Ltd., North Sydney
Prentice-Hall of Canada, Ltd., Toronto
Prentice-Hall of India Private Ltd., New Delhi
Prentice-Hall of Japan, Inc., Tokyo

10   9   8   7   6   5   4   3   2

Library of Congress Cataloging in Publication Data

McTwigan, Michael.
    Clay play.

    SUMMARY: Suggests numerous games and projects with
clay which involve varied degrees of skill.
    1. Educational games—Juvenile literature.
2. Modeling—Juvenile literature. [1. Clay modeling]
I. Post, Henry, joint author. II. Martin, Diane,
illus. III. Title.
LB1140.5.G3M3   372.1'3   72-7277
ISBN 0-13-136408-1

Contents

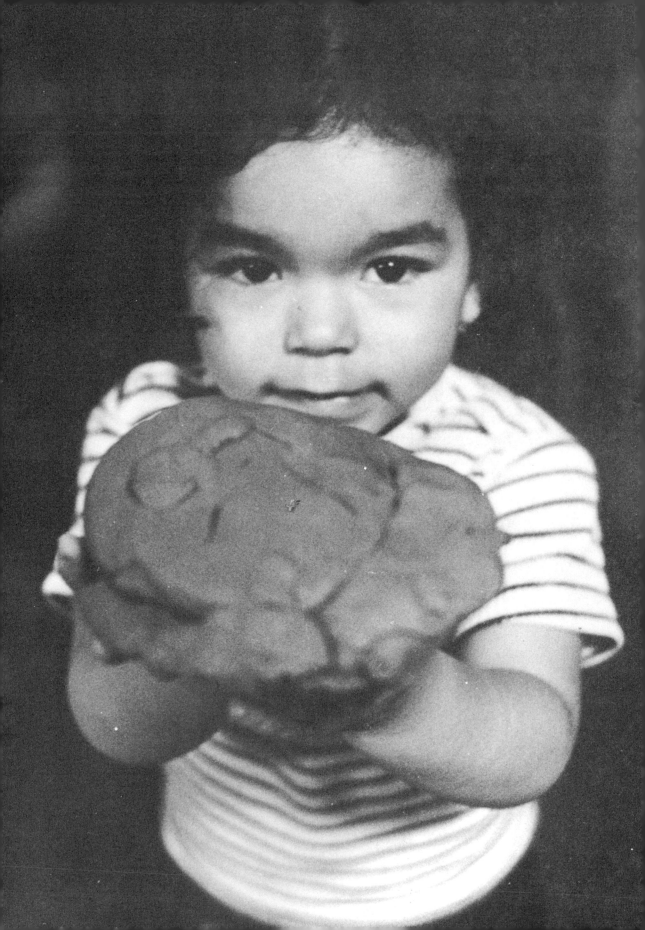

Squeeze Me

Fat Fingers

Stick a ball of clay onto your finger.
What do you have? A fat finger. How
many fat fingers can you have at once?

Stop Laughing

Make a clay ball. Then form a circle with your friends. Throw the ball into the air. As soon as the ball leaves your hand, everyone start laughing. Stop as soon as the ball hits the ground. Can you do it?

Snake Stretch

You can make a snake by rolling a clay ball back and forth. But how long and skinny can you make your snake before he falls apart?

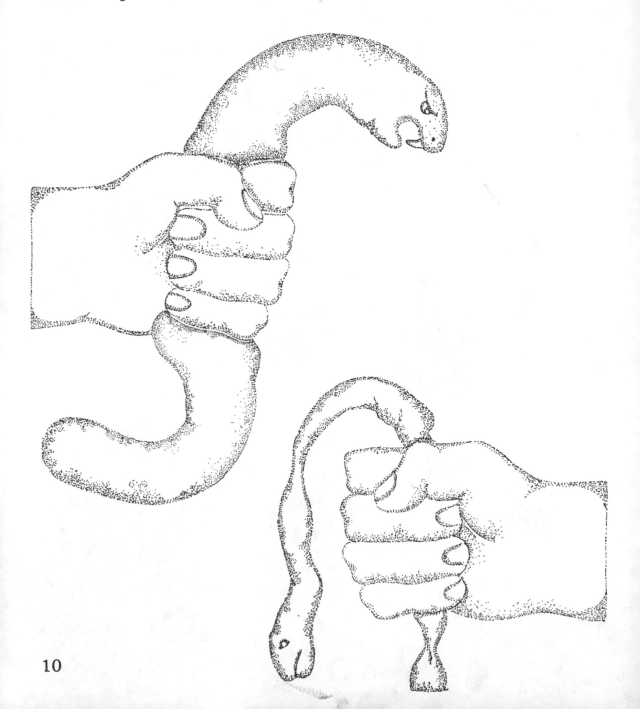

Changes

Make a clay ball and squeeze it until it changes shape into a cube. Now see if you can make it into a pyramid. Then a cylinder. Make as many shapes as you can, one after the other.

Stick It In

Take anything—a block or a fork, for
example—and stick it in your clay. Take
it away and look at the mark you made.
What other things can make clay marks
and designs?

Thick & Thin

Press a big piece of clay into a flat thin slab. Cut it up into squares with a table knife. Pile the squares on top of one another until you have a cube. Keep adding squares. What shapes can your cube turn into?

1.

2.

Fatso & Skinny

How fat can you make a clay person before his stomach hits the ground? How tall and skinny can you make him before he falls down?

House Parts

What shape is a door? What shape is a door knob, a window, a wall, a roof, or a floor? What clay shapes will add up to a house just like yours?

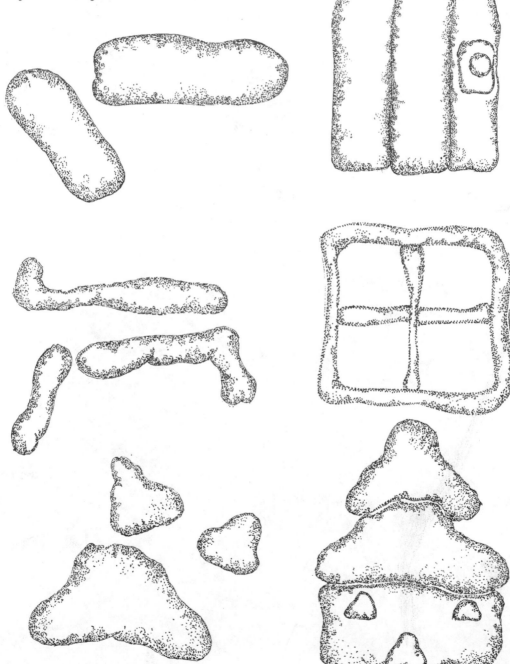

Puzzles

Pound some clay into a flat slab. Cut it into pieces like a jigsaw puzzle with a table knife. Mix up your puzzle pieces and give them to a friend. Can he put it back together again?

Teasers

Shape a hunk of clay into a simple shape like a ball or a cube. Then cut it into a few pieces with a table knife. Mix up the pieces and ask your friend to try to put this puzzle together.

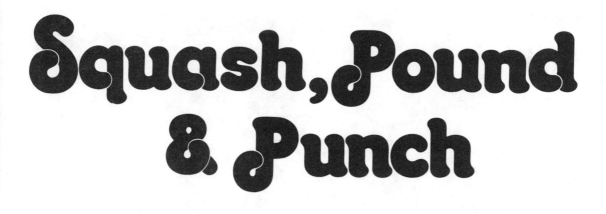

Squash, Pound & Punch

Crazy Shapes

How would you play a game of marbles
if the marbles were square? Would your
glass of milk spill if its bottom was round?
How many crazy things can you make?

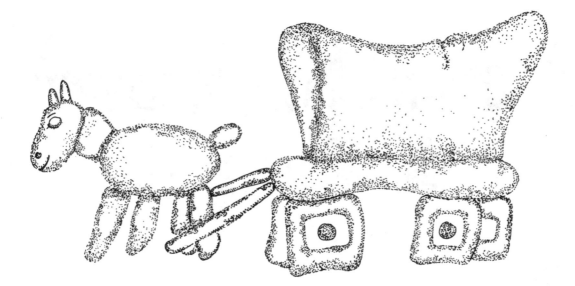

Body Parts

What would people look like if they had legs on their heads? Noses on their knees? What silly bodies can you make?

12 Balls

Make a dozen clay balls—all different sizes. Put them together to make something. Then take them apart and rearrange your clay balls into something else. How many different things can you make out of the clay balls?

Avalanche

Build two different hills, one high and one low. Put a small clay ball at the top of each hill and give it a push. Which hill does the ball roll down fastest?

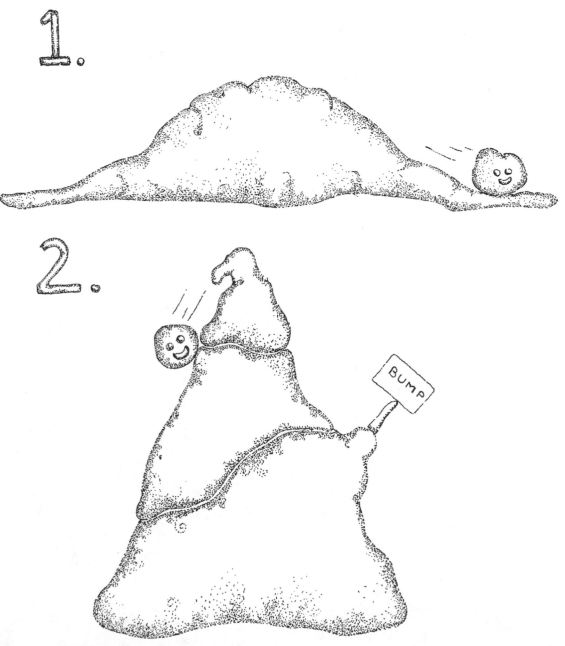

1.

2.

BUMP

Five Friends

You have five very good friends right on the end of your fingers. To make them come alive just give them clay heads and faces.

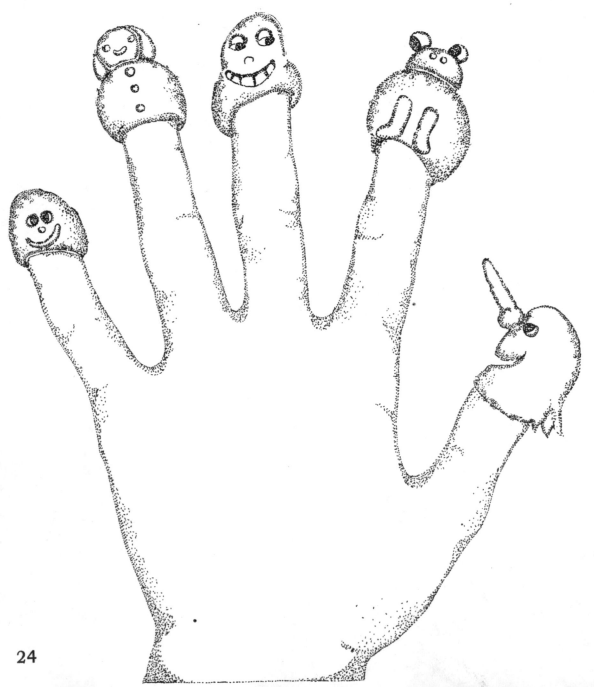

Make a lot of clay balls. Count them and then pile them up. Ask your friends to guess how many balls are in the pile. Can they tell?

25

Spy

How different can you look in glasses? With a big nose? Try hiding under a clay disguise. Can your friends tell it's you?

Silly Letters

How silly can you make the letter "A" look? The letter "B"? How about "C"? Can your friends tell what your crazy letters are supposed to be?

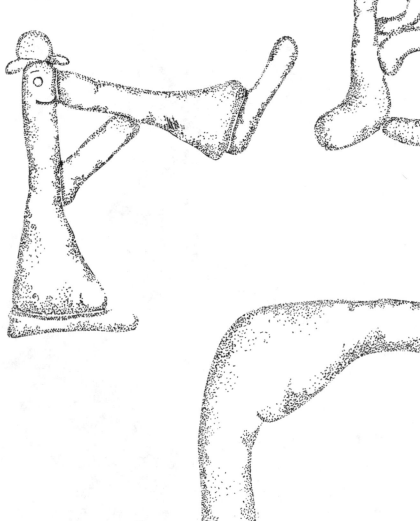

Blind Man's Bluff

Make a clay shape. Blindfold a friend and ask him to feel your clay shape. Now take off his blindfold and ask him to make the same shape without looking at yours. Now you try it.

What Am I Saying

What do you look like when you're happy? When you're sad? Can you make a clay face that says, "I'm happy"? What else can your clay faces say?

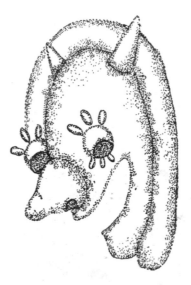

Taking Turns

You and a friend can build the craziest animal in the world if you take turns. You make one part of the animal's body. Your friend makes the next. Keep taking turns. Look at the crazy animal that Mark and Christie made!

Mystery Animal

Think of the animal that you want to build, but don't tell your friend. He thinks of an animal too, but also keeps it a secret. Now taking turns, both of you build *one* animal—the mystery animal.

Bigger & Bigger

Which Is More

Take two clay balls and flatten one. Ask your friends to guess which piece has more clay in it. Roll up the flat piece and they'll see who was right.

Houses

If you lived in Africa or on the North Pole, what would your house be like? How many kinds of houses can you make?

Where Are You

Where is your building, your street, your town? Flatten out a piece of clay and make a map that tells you where you are.

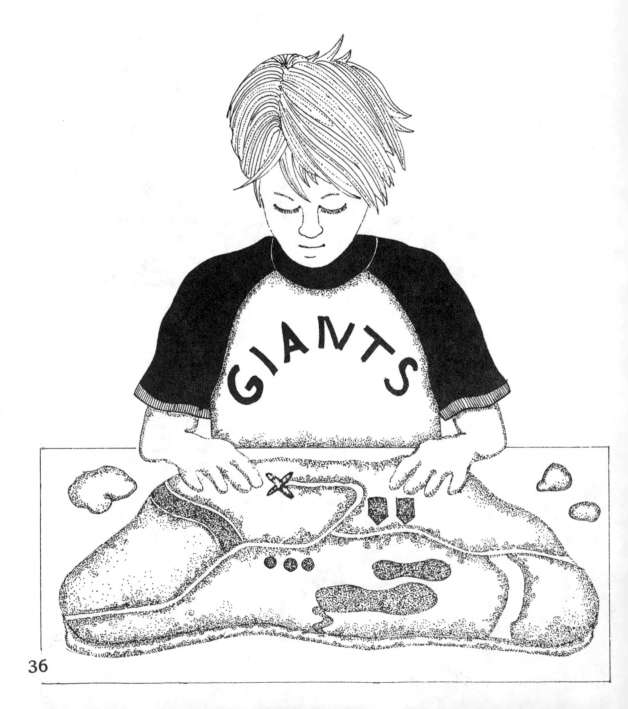

SEEK

Frighten your friends with the scariest
monster you can make.

Traveling

If you wanted to travel a long way, how would you go? Would you drive, or fly, or sail? Think of all the ways you can get from here to there and then make clay models of each.

Which Way

Signs can tell a lot. Your clay signs can show where to go, to stop, to turn left or right, up or down.

39

S Is For Seagull

Try making as many clay things as you can that all begin with the same letter. After that, try another letter.

Your Majesty

Make a clay castle and clay kingdom and you'll become a king or queen. But don't forget your crown.

Your Zoo

There are so many animals in the zoo—
lions and tigers and bears. What animals
will you put in your clay zoo?

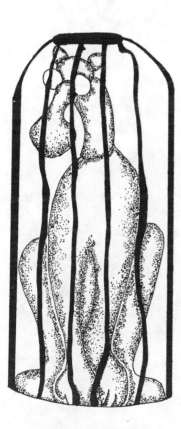
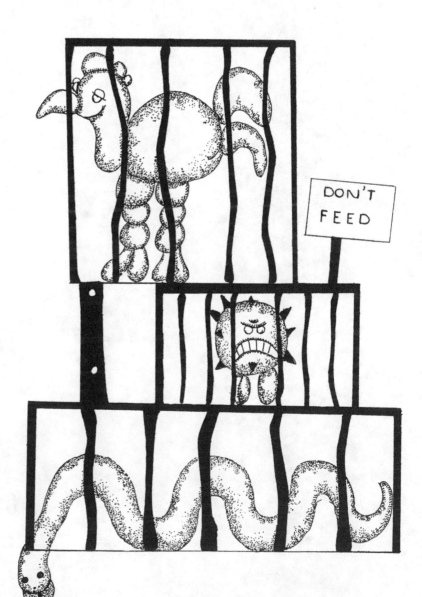

DON'T FEED

Look At This !

Super Market

Make all the foods you like with clay. Compare what you have with your friend's food. Too many apples? Trade some off. Keep trading until you have some of everything.

Goats Have Kids

And so do people. Cows have calves and dogs have puppies. Your clay animals have children too. How many can you make? What are their names?

When I Grow Up

What do you want to be? Try making clay models of you the fireman, or you the movie star. What would you look like as a rock musician? Or a nurse?

In The Beginning

How did the earth begin? From a ball of fire, or a hunk of dust? Then what happened? Try telling the story of the earth's beginning with clay.

Birthday Party

Start making your clay party right away. You better decide what your cake is going to be like. There's lots of clay food and party things you need for all your friends. And don't forget the invitations.

3 Wishes

Suppose you had three wishes. What would they be? Diane wished she could have a banana cream pie for dessert, stay up late, and ride a wild horse. She made models of her wishes and said magic words over them. Think of your wishes, make your models, and try it.

Your Street

How many buildings are there on your street? Where are the sidewalks, the stop signs, and the trees? Can you remember enough about your street to make a clay model?

Good & Bad

Make two things. One that is "Good" and one that is "Bad." What makes good things "Good"? And what makes bad things "Bad"?

 Maze

Some mazes are easy. Others are hard. But the trickiest maze will be the most fun for your friends. Just give them small clay balls and see if they can get through your clay maze.

Hatch Me

Lots of animals come from eggs. Chickens and turtles, snakes and doves. What will you hide in your clay eggs?

Clay City

Imagine the most perfect city in the whole world. What would it be like? How would it work? Try building the clay city you would like to live in.

Notes For Adults

At the rate our culture is changing, most information we can teach a child is likely to be obsolete in a few years' time. What can we teach, then?

The most reasonable thing to teach is the art of discovering and using information. If the child learns that, he will be ready to face an increasingly complex world.

To achieve this goal we must offer an approach to experience that lets the child develop his natural drives for curiosity, for discovery, for relating to the environment. We need to develop new *systems of experience* that will enable the child to organize the changing reality around him in a meaningful way.

The Clay Environment

This book is about clay and the ways clay can be used to help children learn.

Clay is many things, but here we shall look at it only as a medium for providing information. Normally we overlook this unique potential of clay. We let small children mess around with it, hoping that they will derive some pleasure from the experience. We teach older ones to make ashtrays and cups with it, according to *our* specifications.

But clay is much richer than that. It is the "cool" medium *par excellence.* It has many properties to reveal. It can assume any shape we wish. It can do many things. And, as used in the games suggested in this book, clay can help children learn to get along with each other in situations which are neither structured nor completely free. For these reasons, clay is ideal for starting the child on the path to a rich involvement with his environment.

We have learned from Erik Erikson that children between three and eight (to whom this book is directed) have to master three main developmental stages. In each one of these stages, clay has some properties that can be used to help the child master the task appropriate to his age.

1 The child between the ages of three and five is faced with the problem of *autonomy*. His main concern is to learn to manipulate things; he must learn to hold and let go, he must develop a feeling that he can affect and control his environment. For the younger child the meaning of clay is in its malleability; it can be molded and changed easily to fit the child's intentions.

2 About the fourth year, it becomes tremendously important to develop a sense of *initiative,* and a sense of control in the social realm, too; to take charge and to take responsibility for initiating action in concert with others. These clay games allow the child to experiment with interpersonal strategies that require cooperation and initiative.

3 By the time he is eight, a child is confronted with the task of developing a sense of *industry.* Now his self-respect demands that he begin to be competent in the productive world, meeting its standards of accomplishment. He has to feel useful, and respected for his contributions. Here again, clay allows the child to perfect his workmanship and to produce results which will help him cope with the main maturational tasks of his stage of life.

Working with clay gives the child much needed information about *himself.* At this stage clay is better than drawing for making the child aware of his own capabilities. He does not just represent or describe things, he actually makes them. The concrete objectivity of the product is a sign of accomplishment that children rarely get to experience.

There are all too few situations in our culture where a child can get these experiences and learn about his environment at the same time. The present book is a modest attempt to allow children the feeling of competence that comes from making things with their own hands, all within a context of games that will help them to gather information about a limited, but very rich aspect of reality.

Learning & Discovery

One more word is needed, perhaps, to reassure those for whom "games" connotes the opposite of learning. A game is a game if it is fun—an activity meaningful in its own terms and needing no other justification. What better way to insure involvement in a learning situation than making it a game?

Learning is, before anything else, *experiencing.* Not only seeing with the eyes, but feeling, smelling, tasting. Yet much of what we do to children cuts off their efforts to experience, thereby impairing their ability to truly learn. "This is a book, and books are for reading." "Isn't this flower pretty? Flowers are for decoration." By defining objects in the child's environment in *our* terms, the child learns *our* way of experiencing by a short cut which will eventually destroy his openness to experience. And that openness is the most precious asset for learning to face a changing world.

No, books are not for reading only. They have mass, they can be used to keep papers in place, or they can be thrown at the cat. They can be used to hide things, including flowers. Books smell. Their pages have texture which is sometimes pleasant to touch. And so on and so forth. Flowers *are* for decoration, but they are also food to insects and sometimes to man. They smell and feel strange. More than anything else, flowers are independent systems, with their own needs. Children should be allowed and encouraged to discover these things themselves.

How Children Learn

If you tell a child what something is, he won't know it. But if you let him discover it for himself, that will be knowledge. And once he learns to use the process of discovery, he will be onto the way of learning.

When the child discovers a new object he asks, "How is it?" Or, in more learned language, what are its properties? Is it large or small, soft or hard, living or inanimate, moving or still . . . good or bad? When you look at even the most ordinary object with these questions in mind, you suddenly discover how many qualities that old thing has. Then you begin to discover how rich your whole environment is.

Next, "What does it do?" Every object can do much more than what it has been designed for. Children are notorious for finding the most incredible uses for everyday things. They play best and longest with "toys" that are least clearly delimited in what they can do. Unfortunately, we often thwart this tendency. We should encourage it instead and help the child to learn about the many ways things can be.

Another basic facet of learning is to discover how things can *relate to each other*. Placing objects in new contexts reveals the subtle links between the qualities of objects and the ways they work.

Finally, *objects are not only what they already are.* They can become other things. Learning consists of discovering what things are or what they can become. A handful of clay has many properties, it can do many things, it can relate to many other objects, but it can also become something else if we do certain things to it. The process of changing the environment is one of the fundamental elements of learning discovery.

The most important prerequisite for starting the learning process on the right track is to encourage a child's *involvement* with his environment. He has to feel that the objects around him matter. He has to feel that what is happening around him relates to his concerns. He should learn that anything can become an extension of his own self, and he must begin to see himself as an extension of everything else in the world. Without this connecting "ecological consciousness" there is no incentive to really learn about anything in depth.

A good educator should always try to help the child connect what he sees to what matters to him. To do so one must know the child and his concerns. One must show how the things one is trying to teach will affect the experiences the child cares about.

How Not To Get Trapped

No book can teach learning. It would be sad if this book, which was put together to encourage discovery, were to be used to squelch it. It must be remembered that information is subjective: a fact is information only if it is perceived as such. It is a child who knows what is worth learning.

We can only suggest ways for him to look, to compare, to relate. But we should not be surprised if he goes his own way and sees things differently from how we hope him to. It is *his* learning. Our task is done when we have presented, to the best of our knowledge, the ideal conditions for learning how to discover and use information.

Mihalyi Csikszentmihalyi,
Committee on Human Development, University of Chicago

Clay

There are many different types of clay, but any modeling or pottery clay will work well for the games in this book. Oil-based modeling clay is widely available in dime stores and toy stores. It will not dry out, but *is* expensive and sold only in small quantities. Pottery clay is far cheaper and is usually sold in resealable plastic bags of ten pounds or more. When your children have finished playing with the clay, be sure to return it to the bag so that it will not dry out. Of course, after the clay is handled for a while, it does lose moisture and becomes stiff, and hard to work. So, it is best to wet the clay after every use. Flatten the clay out, press your thumb into it, making small depressions or "wells," and pour water on it. To work the water into the clay, knead it as you would bread. Hold it with both hands, press it against the table, and push it away from you at the same time. Then roll the clay back toward you and press again. If the clay is still too stiff to squeeze easily after kneading for a minute, flatten it again, add more water, and knead it until it is uniformly moist.

Clay is a popular medium in elementary school art classes and most art teachers can direct you to a source of clay. Looking in the yellow pages of the phone book, under the following headings, will also lead you to a supplier: "Clay," "Ceramic Equipment and Supplies," "Arts and Crafts Supplies," or "Artist's Materials and Supplies." If you find nothing in the phone book, call the art department of a nearby college, university, or art school. And if they can't help you, write to us and we'll put you in touch with some clay.

Game Index